This book is dedicated to

Donnie "Yooperman" Stefanski
The best dad, husband, grandpa, uncle and friend.
A true fan of fans.

FORD FIE
365 MILE

and the

adventure

begins…

Yooperman lived 365 miles

from his football team.

His love of football carried over

to the friends he made

by traveling to watch them on Sundays.

He traveled the 10 hours

every Sunday to see

his team and football family.

Many friends met up to

tailgate before the games.

The Pilgrims loved the

Thanksgiving game the best.

They became family to

Yooperman and Yoopergirl.

Being a Superfan introduces you to

many new friends.

Yooperman and Crackman

were the best of friends.

They met up every Sunday

to cheer on their team

and have fun with

other fans,

no matter the team.

Every halftime was a meet up at the Pop Pole.

This was a meeting place set up

by Yoop and Crack and

other Superfans joined in.

Yoopergirl and LionEyes

like to take coin shots when they met up.

Their coins symbolize their love of football,

fans and charity.

Traveling to away games

is a fun season tradition.

Meeting up with other

fans of teams

makes you realize

that football equals family.

Yooperman and Crackman

had a great day

celebrating their win

in the Land of Cheese.

Their yearly road trips

were always filled

with funny stories

and great times.

LionMane and LionEyes

were a part of the family as well.

They issued a coin to Yoopergirl

for her to join their Superfan family.

Being a part of the group

that Yooperman was inducted to

meant a lot.

Every August, the Superfans

meet up in Ohio

to celebrate another season.

They will always miss Yooperman,

but they will always

be a family.

Being fans, supporting charity

and showing loyalty

will always be how they show

they are members of the pride.

Megan Stefanski

She is a Lions Superfan from the Upper Peninsula of Michigan. She travels to every Lions game and each home game is 365 miles each way. She leaves at 2:30am and returns home around 11pm each Sunday.

She is a school librarian and also works at her family restaurant- Yooperman's Bar and Grill.

Made in the USA
Monee, IL
20 September 2023

43089463R00021